We Are All One

By Juan Carlos

We are all one.
The earth revolves around the sun.

The earth among the stars.
The stars across the galaxy.

Not far off is Mars.

The universe too big to see.

Wherever you are, you open your eyes.

You rise from your bed to see the blue skies.

Even when they are cloudy and gray.
Just go with the flow and start a new day!

Different people live in different places.

With all kinds of lives and all kinds of faces.

Don't think for a second we're not connected.
From people in Baghdad to people in Texas.

It's time for breakfast all the world over.

Bacon and bagels and biscuits and butter.

Some like it hotter and some like it colder.

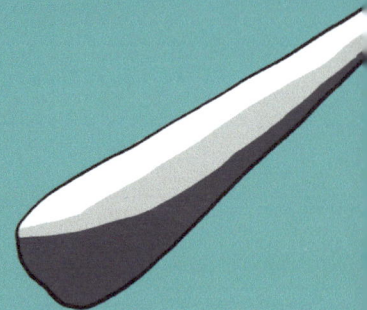

Salmon and scones and strudel and strata.

Work or play or getting an education,

we do the same things in every nation.

Listen to music
and lay back for an hour,

or stroll through the park
and smell a new flower.

Or have a coffee with a long lost friend.

Or read a good book until the end.

Before long, it's afternoon
and dinner will be ready soon.

Get in the car, go home, you're late.
Thankfully, they saved you a plate.

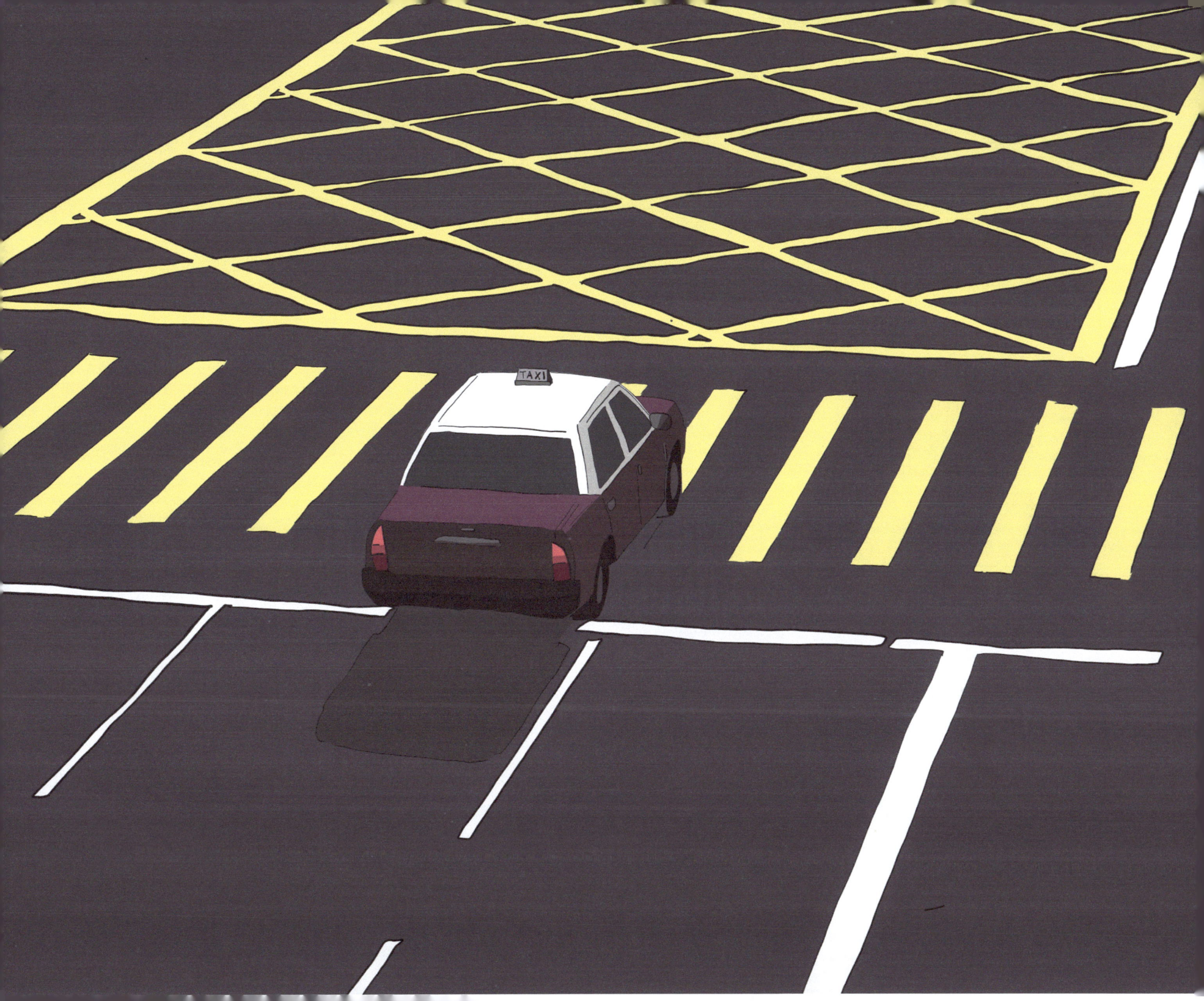

At dusk we all see the setting sun,
and reflect on all the things we have done.

From people in China to people in France,
we wish on the stars, we dream of romance.

Mindfulness to relax your head.

Eyes droopy, big yawn, it's time for bed.

Brush those teeth and get in your pajamas.
Instead of counting sheep, try counting llamas.

Finally, dreamland is near.

One last thought becomes crystal clear.

Son or daughter or father or mother,
Our time is a gift, and we love one another.

Around and around on this giant sphere.

Day after day and year after year.

Living here together as one.

We all revolve around the sun.

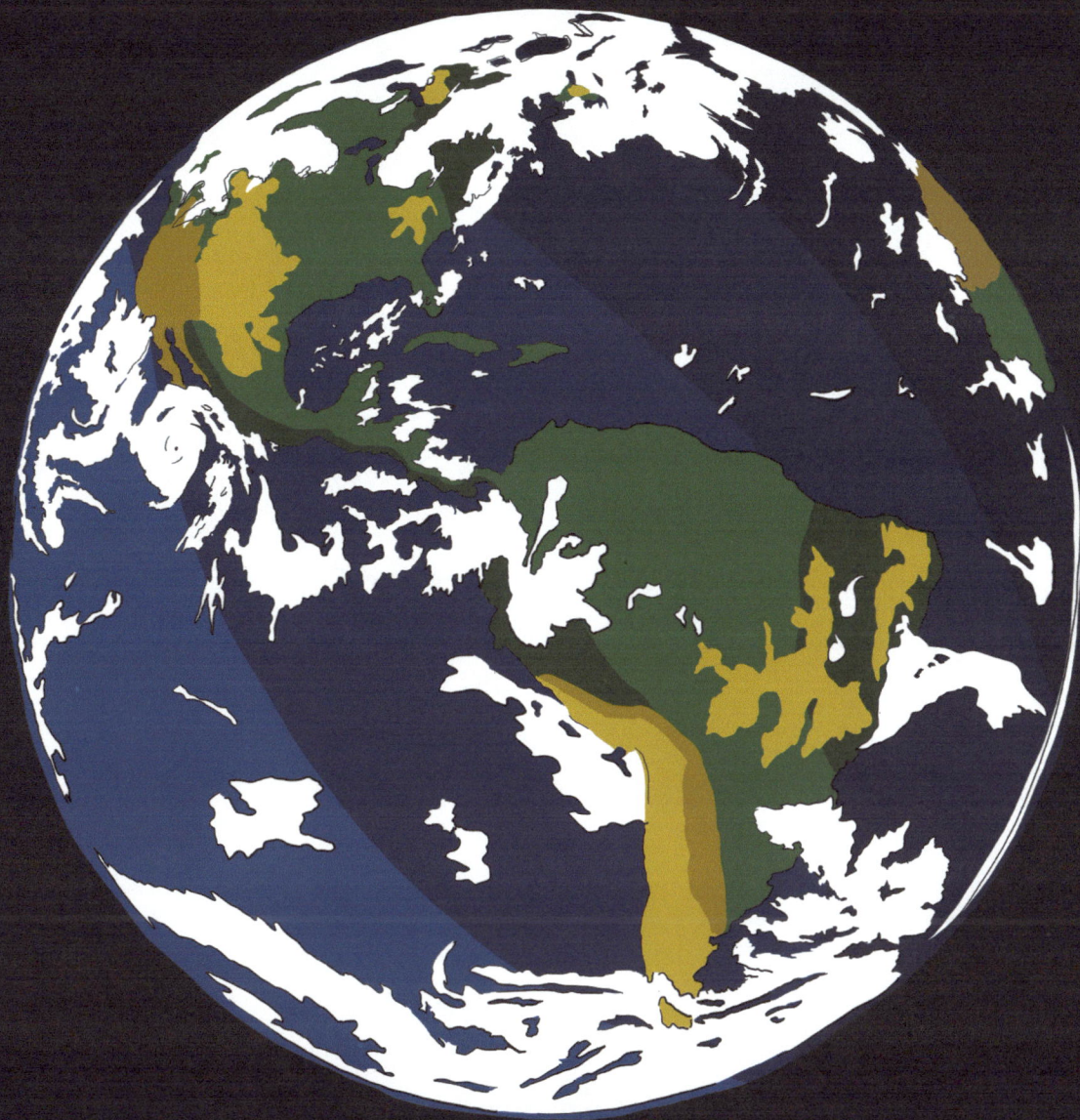

When Juan Carlos was a kid, his favorite book was Caps For Sale. There was something fun about wearing so many hats. When he got older, he realized the appeal: he loves wearing lots of hats! The most important one, father to two amazing children. They live in the desert together, where they marvel at the world around them.

www.ingramcontent.com/pod-product-compliance
Lightning Source LLC
Chambersburg PA
CBHW040713150426

42811CB00062B/1880